MAYER SMITH

Falling for the Shadowed Billionaire

Copyright © 2025 by Mayer Smith

All rights reserved. No part of this publication may be reproduced, stored or transmitted in any form or by any means, electronic, mechanical, photocopying, recording, scanning, or otherwise without written permission from the publisher. It is illegal to copy this book, post it to a website, or distribute it by any other means without permission.

This novel is entirely a work of fiction. The names, characters and incidents portrayed in it are the work of the author's imagination. Any resemblance to actual persons, living or dead, events or localities is entirely coincidental.

Mayer Smith asserts the moral right to be identified as the author of this work.

Mayer Smith has no responsibility for the persistence or accuracy of URLs for external or third-party Internet Websites referred to in this publication and does not guarantee that any content on such Websites is, or will remain, accurate or appropriate.

Designations used by companies to distinguish their products are often claimed as trademarks. All brand names and product names used in this book and on its cover are trade names, service marks, trademarks and registered trademarks of their respective owners. The publishers and the book are not associated with any product or vendor mentioned in this book. None of the companies referenced within the book have endorsed the book.

First edition

This book was professionally typeset on Reedsy. Find out more at reedsy.com

Contents

1	A Life of Luxury	1
2	The Escape	7
3	New Beginnings	13
4	The Mysterious Stranger	19
5	An Unlikely Friendship	25
6	Shared Secrets	31
7	A Glimpse Into His World	37
8	The Reveal	44
9	Confrontation	51
10	A Difficult Decision	58
11	Breaking the Walls	65
12	The Tipping Point	72
13	Letting Go of the Past	79
14	Building a Future	86
15	A Love That Transcends	93

One

A Life of Luxury

T he sound of heels clicking against the marble floor echoed through the grand hallway of the mansion. It was a sound that had become so familiar to Sophia Bennett over the years, a sound that marked her entrance into a world she had grown to resent but could never escape. The mansion, perched high on a hill overlooking the city, was a symbol of everything her family had built—wealth, power, and influence. But to Sophia, it was nothing more than a gilded cage, a prison of expectations and responsibilities that suffocated her every day.

Sophia paused at the top of the staircase, looking down at the sprawling estate that had been her home for as long as she could remember. The chandeliers sparkled above, casting an ethereal glow across the polished floors, while the walls were lined with priceless artwork, each piece a testament to the family's fortune. Yet, none of it brought her comfort. None of it filled the emptiness inside her.

She ran a hand through her long, dark hair, her fingers brushing against the soft silk of her gown. The dress was the finest in the city, custom-made by a designer who had catered to her family's every whim for years. The fabric clung to her curves, its rich color reflecting her social status, but she felt nothing as she stood there. No joy, no excitement—only a sense of obligation. Another event. Another night of pretending.

Tonight was no different. The annual Bennett Gala was in full swing, a glittering affair that brought together the most powerful people in the city. Business tycoons, political figures, celebrities—they all mingled in the opulent ballroom, their laughter and clinking glasses filling the air. To the outside world, it was the epitome of luxury, a celebration of success and privilege. But to Sophia, it was just another night of being on display, another night of being the perfect daughter of the perfect family.

She took a deep breath and descended the staircase, her footsteps measured and graceful. Her mother, standing at the bottom, was already waiting for her. Diane Bennett was everything Sophia had been groomed to be—a picture of elegance, poise, and charm. Her mother's blonde hair was perfectly styled, and her dress shimmered under the light, just like Sophia's. There was no question that Diane was the queen of the evening, the centerpiece of the gala, and she expected nothing less from her daughter.

A Life of Luxury

"Sophia," her mother greeted her with a practiced smile. "You look stunning, darling. The guests will be thrilled to see you."

Sophia forced a smile, her lips curving upward in the way she knew was expected. "Thank you, Mother."

Diane surveyed her daughter with a critical eye, adjusting the collar of Sophia's gown. "Remember, tonight is important. The board members will be here, as will several potential investors. You need to make a good impression. The future of Bennett Enterprises depends on it."

Sophia nodded, her mind already drifting elsewhere. Bennett Enterprises. Her family's legacy. The company that had made them billionaires, and the weight of responsibility that had been placed on her shoulders since the day she was born. It was all a game to them—one she had played far too long.

As they walked into the ballroom together, Sophia's heart sank. The room was filled with laughter, clinking glasses, and the murmur of polished conversations. The men were in tuxedos, the women in sparkling gowns, and everywhere she looked, there was someone eager to speak to her mother. Diane was the queen of this social scene, as always. And Sophia was nothing more than her dutiful princess, standing by her side, smiling, nodding, pretending to care.

"Go mingle, darling," Diane instructed, her voice smooth and commanding. "I'll be over here with the Harringtons."

Sophia didn't argue. She had learned long ago that it was easier to follow orders than to question them. With a polite smile, she excused herself from her mother and wandered into the crowd. The glass of champagne in her hand was cold, but she didn't drink it. She had learned to hide her distaste for the world she was born into, and this was one of those nights when the mask had to stay firmly in place.

She moved through the room, exchanging pleasantries with guests she barely knew. Her attention drifted from one person to the next, each conversation as meaningless as the last. Her mind was elsewhere, thinking about the life she had left behind—or rather, the life she had run from. The life where she was free.

But that freedom had come at a cost.

Her phone buzzed in her pocket, and she quickly glanced at the screen, expecting a message from her assistant. But it wasn't from work. It was a text from an old friend, someone she hadn't heard from in years.

"Are you happy, Sophia? I miss you. You deserve more than this."

The message sent a wave of unease through her, the words echoing in her mind. She missed her old life too. The one before all the wealth, the pressure, and the suffocating expectations. She missed the simplicity of her days in Paris, the freedom to walk down the street without being recognized, the ability to make decisions without considering the opinions of the board or her mother.

A Life of Luxury

But that life was gone. She had traded it for this—luxury, fame, and a gilded cage.

She sighed and tucked the phone back into her clutch, trying to shake off the feeling of being trapped. But it lingered, gnawing at her insides. And then, as if the universe had heard her silent plea, she saw him.

Across the room, standing by the far corner, was a man who seemed entirely out of place. His dark, brooding demeanor contrasted sharply with the gleaming smiles and sparkling gowns of the guests around him. He was dressed in an impeccable suit, but there was something about the way he stood that screamed rebellion, as if he were completely uninterested in the world that surrounded him.

Sophia's curiosity piqued. Who was he? She had never seen him before, and he certainly didn't look like the usual crowd of rich businessmen who attended the gala. His piercing blue eyes scanned the room with a detached air, as if he were observing rather than participating in the spectacle.

Their gazes locked for a brief moment, and Sophia felt a jolt in her chest. There was something about him—something different. Something that made her question the life she had so carefully curated.

But just as quickly as it had started, the moment passed, and the man turned away, slipping into the shadows of the room. Sophia stood frozen for a moment, her heart racing. What was it about him? Why had he made her feel like that?

She didn't know the answer, but for the first time in years, a spark of something real—something unexpected—had been ignited inside her. And she wasn't sure whether it would be the beginning of something beautiful or the destruction of the life she had built.

Two

The Escape

The car door slammed shut behind Sophia, the sound reverberating through the crisp, cold air. She didn't turn to look at the mansion as the driver revved the engine and pulled away from the driveway. She couldn't. Every time she glanced back, it felt like the weight of her family's legacy was clawing at her, dragging her back to a life she could no longer endure.

Her hands gripped the leather seat beneath her, her knuckles white. The city lights blurred outside the window, each streetlamp flickering by like a ghostly reminder of the life she was leaving behind. But it wasn't enough to stop the tightness in her chest, the knot of anxiety that seemed to grow tighter with every mile. She had made the decision, and there was no going back now.

The streets of the city blurred into the distant countryside as the car sped away, leaving behind the glittering skyline and the towering buildings that had always made her feel small. Sophia leaned her head against the window, staring out at the passing landscape, her mind racing.

Where would she go? What would she do?

She had no plan, no concrete idea of what her life would look like beyond the walls of the Bennett mansion. The only thing she knew was that she couldn't breathe in that suffocating world any longer. She had spent her whole life playing the part of the dutiful daughter, the perfect socialite, the trophy heir to her family's vast fortune. But none of it had ever felt real. None of it had ever been her choice.

For years, her parents had made decisions for her. Her mother had arranged her social calendar, her father had dictated her future, and every step she took had been carefully monitored to ensure that she remained in line with the image they had crafted for her. The gala last night was just another example of their control. It had been an exhausting charade, a night of smiling through clenched teeth and enduring conversations with people who only cared about her family's wealth, never about who she truly was.

The thought of spending another night in that world made her feel trapped, suffocated by the expectations that hung over her like a dark cloud. She couldn't do it anymore. So, she had left.

Sophia's gaze drifted to the rearview mirror, watching the

The Escape

taillights of the car ahead disappear into the darkness. For the first time in her life, she felt a surge of freedom. It was a terrifying, exhilarating feeling—a sense of release she had never known. But it was also terrifying because she had no idea where it would lead.

She closed her eyes, trying to quiet the chaos in her mind. She didn't want to think about the future. She didn't want to think about what she was leaving behind. All she wanted was to escape the prison she had built for herself.

The driver slowed the car as they approached a small town, the faint glow of streetlights illuminating the sleepy streets. Sophia straightened in her seat, her curiosity piqued. This was where she would start. She didn't know why, but something about the place felt right. It was quiet. Simple. The kind of place where people lived without the pressure of status or wealth hanging over them.

The car turned onto a narrow street, passing by small cottages with flower boxes hanging from the windows. Sophia noticed a small café on the corner, its warm light spilling out onto the sidewalk. For a brief moment, she felt as though she had stepped into another world—one where no one cared who her family was, one where no one knew her name.

The car stopped in front of a modest, two-story house. The driver got out and opened the door for her. Sophia stepped out, taking in the crisp night air, the scent of freshly mown grass and earth filling her lungs. It was different here. It was real. And it felt like home, even though it wasn't.

"This is it," the driver said, handing her a small key. "Your new home."

Sophia took the key, her fingers trembling slightly as she grasped it. She hadn't told anyone where she was going. Her family wouldn't understand. Her mother would insist on bringing her back, and her father would see her actions as nothing more than a childish tantrum. They had never understood the weight of the life she was living. They had never understood her need to break free.

But this was her decision. Her choice. And she was finally taking control.

The driver gave her a nod before returning to the car and driving off into the night, leaving Sophia standing alone in front of the house. She stood there for a moment, taking in the quiet stillness of the night, the soft rustling of leaves in the trees overhead. It felt peaceful here, like the world was slowing down for the first time in years.

Sophia pushed open the door and stepped inside, her footsteps echoing in the empty house. It was small, nothing like the grand mansion she had grown up in. But it was enough. She could make it work. She wasn't sure what she was going to do next, but she would figure it out. One step at a time.

The house was sparsely furnished, a simple couch, a coffee table, and a small kitchen area in the corner. There was nothing extravagant about it. Nothing to remind her of the life she had left behind. The walls were bare, and the air was thick with the

The Escape

scent of dust. But it was hers.

She dropped her purse onto the counter and walked over to the window, peering out at the quiet street. It was still early, but the town seemed to be winding down for the night. A few people walked past the window, their footsteps muffled by the distance. She felt an overwhelming sense of peace in the simplicity of it all. This was what she had been searching for—the freedom to be herself, without the weight of her family's expectations.

Her phone buzzed in her pocket, snapping her out of her reverie. She pulled it out and glanced at the screen. The message was from her mother.

"Where are you, Sophia? This is ridiculous. Come back home. You have responsibilities."

Sophia's heart sank. She knew this was coming. Her mother would never understand. She couldn't. It wasn't just about running away. It was about breaking free from the chains of a life she never wanted.

Sophia typed out a quick reply: "I'm fine. I'm where I need to be."

She hit send, then tossed the phone onto the couch. It was time to stop thinking about her old life. She had made her choice. And now, for the first time in years, she was going to live it.

With a deep breath, she turned away from the window, her mind racing with the possibilities of what the future might hold. For the first time, she didn't feel like she was playing a role. She was simply a woman who had made a choice—a woman free from the life she had been born into.

And she was ready for whatever came next.

Three

New Beginnings

Sophia stood in front of the cracked mirror in the small bathroom of her new home, staring at the reflection of a woman she barely recognized. Her hair, once perfectly styled and immaculately done for endless gala events, now hung in soft waves around her face, unbrushed, untamed. The flawless makeup she had once applied daily was nowhere to be found. In its place was a tired expression, eyes that carried a weight she hadn't realized had settled there. The past was still fresh, looming like a shadow over her new life. She didn't know yet whether this decision was the right one or if she was simply running from something too powerful to escape.

A small, tired laugh escaped her lips as she turned from the mirror, shaking her head. Who am I kidding? she thought. This is all so new, so uncertain. I'm nothing but a stranger to this world.

She was alone in this new town, a town where no one knew the Bennett name. It was her first true taste of anonymity in years. There was no family name to live up to, no high-profile events where her presence was expected, and no business partners or investors who could cast judgment on her every move. The only thing that mattered now was what she chose to make of this new life. But even now, there was that nagging voice in her head—her mother's words, her father's expectations, and the pressure to be perfect. It felt like the weight of her old life clung to her despite the vastness of her new freedom.

But she had to push that aside. For the first time in her life, she was going to do things her way.

With a deep breath, Sophia reached for the fraying towel hanging from the hook. She dried her face, the cold water invigorating her as if it were washing away not just the dirt, but the ghosts of her past. She hadn't made any decisions about her next move, but she knew one thing for certain: she couldn't stay cooped up in this house forever. She needed to step out, to see the world outside her door, to feel like she wasn't hiding, even from herself.

The street outside her window was quiet—much quieter than anything she had ever known. No honking horns, no traffic that never stopped, no noise that bled into her thoughts. Just a small town, still under the blanket of the night. A few lights flickered on the other side of the road, a solitary lamp post casting a soft, golden glow on the pavement.

Sophia's heart thudded in her chest as she gathered the courage

New Beginnings

to step out of the house. She grabbed her jacket and slid it over her shoulders, walking out of the front door and onto the porch. The air was cool, carrying with it the earthy scent of pine trees and damp soil. It was everything she had imagined—simple, unassuming, and full of the promise of a fresh start.

The little town was exactly what she had been looking for. But as her shoes met the pavement, the unease began to settle in. This wasn't just about escaping her old life; it was about building something new, from the ground up. But what if she wasn't capable of it? What if she was too broken, too accustomed to the life of luxury she had left behind?

Stop it, she told herself. You're here because you wanted something more, something real. And you're going to make it work. One step at a time.

The streets of the town were quieter than she had imagined. Small shops lined the main road, their windows dark and empty now, but she could imagine them bustling with life during the day. There was a sense of warmth in the stillness, a sense of belonging she hadn't felt in years. People were real here, not concerned with wealth or the brand of clothes they wore or whose name was on the guest list at the latest social gathering.

As she walked further down the road, she passed a cozy little bookstore, its windows stacked with books, each one promising an escape into another world. Her eyes lingered on the faded sign above the door: The Whispering Pages. She smiled softly. It had been years since she'd last picked up a book for leisure, lost in the tide of work and appearances. But here, in this town, she didn't have to be anyone but herself.

She pushed open the door, a soft bell chiming above her head as she entered. The scent of paper and ink immediately enveloped her, an oddly comforting smell. The store was small but quaint, its wooden shelves filled with books of all kinds, from old classics to contemporary novels. A few patrons sat at small tables in the back, quietly flipping through pages, lost in their own worlds.

The woman behind the counter looked up from a book she was reading and smiled warmly. "Good evening. How can I help you?"

Sophia blinked, slightly caught off guard by the friendly tone. "Just looking," she said, her voice still a little distant as she walked deeper into the store.

It felt nice to be just another person, to not be seen as a celebrity or an heiress with a legacy weighing her down. Here, she was just another customer, another person in search of a good story. For the first time in a long time, she felt like she could breathe.

She wandered the aisles, her fingers lightly grazing the spines of the books, until one caught her eye—a title she couldn't quite place. She pulled it from the shelf and examined it closely. The Simple Life: How to Find Peace in a World of Chaos. It seemed almost too fitting, like it had been waiting for her. She hesitated for a moment before placing it in her arms and walking to the counter.

New Beginnings

The woman behind the counter raised an eyebrow but said nothing, simply ringing up the book. "Is this your first time in town?" she asked, her voice laced with curiosity.

Sophia nodded. "Yes, I just moved here."

The woman smiled, handing her the bag with the book inside. "Well, welcome. If you ever need a place to escape, this is it."

Sophia smiled back, the warmth of the gesture making her feel like maybe, just maybe, this could be the beginning of something new. "Thanks," she said softly, before slipping out of the store and into the night.

As she walked back down the quiet street, she couldn't shake the feeling that something was watching her. She glanced over her shoulder, but the street behind her was empty. It's just your imagination, she thought, shaking her head. Still, there was something unsettling about the idea of being so completely anonymous. In her old life, the eyes of the world were always on her. She had grown used to it, even though she loathed it. But here, in this town, she felt like she could disappear—like no one would care.

That thought should have been comforting. But it wasn't. It felt lonely.

She stopped by a bench near the park, sitting down and pulling her knees up to her chest. The book was still in her bag, but for now, she just needed to think. She needed to find a way to stop the constant feeling of dread that seemed to haunt her thoughts.

In the distance, she heard a faint sound—the crunch of gravel underfoot, the faint rustle of leaves being disturbed. She turned sharply, her heart racing. A figure emerged from the shadows of the park, their movements deliberate, purposeful.

Sophia's breath caught in her throat as she recognized him.

The man from the gala.

He stood a few yards away, his eyes locked on hers with an intensity that made her pulse race. He hadn't seen her in this town before—she was sure of it. Yet there he was, as if fate had brought him into her life again.

The man who despised wealth. The man who had made her heart race for reasons she couldn't explain.

What was he doing here? And why did the sight of him unsettle her more than it should?

Four

The Mysterious Stranger

Sophia's breath caught in her chest as the figure slowly emerged from the shadows of the park. Her pulse quickened, her thoughts colliding in a whirl of confusion and unease. The man she had seen at the gala, the man who had stood apart from the crowd, was now standing just a few yards away from her. His sharp, chiseled features were now more distinct in the dim light, but his dark eyes were still as unreadable as they had been that night.

She instinctively stood up from the bench, her hand gripping the bag that held the book she had just purchased. She felt a strange urge to flee, to turn and run back to the safety of her new home, but something rooted her to the spot. The night air was crisp, carrying with it a quiet tension that seemed to pulse between them. He hadn't said a word, hadn't moved an inch, but there was something in his gaze—something that made her feel as though he could see right through her.

She took a step back, trying to compose herself, but her voice faltered as she spoke. "What are you doing here?" she asked, her words barely more than a whisper, as though the question were not just aimed at him, but at herself as well. Why am I asking? she thought. Why do I care?

The man's lips curved into a faint, almost imperceptible smirk. "Is it so strange for a person to be in a park?" His voice was low, gravelly, with a hint of something dark beneath the surface. It wasn't just the words; it was the way he said them, as though he were mocking the very question.

Sophia swallowed hard, trying to steady her breath, but she couldn't shake the feeling that he wasn't just a random passerby. There was something deliberate in the way he had appeared. Something intentional. She had no idea how he had found her, but she couldn't deny that his presence here felt too much like fate.

"I... I didn't expect to see you again," Sophia said, her voice more composed now, though her heart was still racing. "I thought you didn't like this world."

He raised an eyebrow, the faintest glimmer of amusement flickering in his eyes. "And what world would that be?" he asked, his gaze narrowing slightly as if he were studying her more intently now.

"The world of wealth, luxury," she replied, a little more boldly

The Mysterious Stranger

than she had intended. "The kind of world I come from."

The man took a step closer, his movements smooth, almost predatory. He didn't seem to hurry, but his presence grew more overwhelming with each inch he closed between them. He wasn't physically imposing, but there was a certain energy about him—a quiet, dangerous intensity—that made her feel small and vulnerable in his presence.

"You think you know me," he said, his voice low and controlled. "You don't."

Sophia felt her stomach twist. There was a bite in his tone, something more than just an observation. It was a warning. She didn't know whether to be offended or intrigued, but she couldn't tear her gaze away from his.

"Then who are you?" she asked, the question slipping out before she could stop herself. "I mean, I saw you at the gala. You don't seem like the kind of person who belongs there."

The man's lips twitched into a tight smile. "I belong nowhere. Least of all in that world."

Sophia felt a shiver run down her spine. His words were heavy, as though they carried more than just disdain for her world. She didn't understand why he would come to the gala if he so vehemently despised it, but it didn't feel like the right time to ask more questions. Instead, she found herself drawn to him, to the mystery of who he was and why he seemed so familiar to her.

"Why are you following me?" she asked, her voice barely audible now. Her heart was pounding in her chest, each beat louder than the last.

He didn't answer right away. Instead, he stepped closer still, and she could feel the pull of his presence like a gravitational force she couldn't escape. He stopped just a few feet from her, his gaze unwavering.

"I'm not following you," he said quietly, his eyes never leaving hers. "But you're hiding something."

Sophia's breath caught in her throat. There it was again—his unsettling ability to make her feel as though she were being scrutinized, laid bare before him. It was as though he could see into the deepest corners of her soul, know things she hadn't even admitted to herself.

"What do you mean?" she asked, her voice shaking despite her attempt to sound composed.

He tilted his head slightly, studying her with that same penetrating gaze. "You left everything behind," he said softly, his voice taking on a darker tone. "But you still carry it with you. That life. That name. It's in the way you carry yourself, in the way you speak. You're not fooling anyone."

Sophia recoiled as though he had slapped her. The words stung, hitting too close to home. She had spent the last few days in this town, trying to convince herself that she was starting over, that the world she had left behind would be nothing more than a distant memory. But now, standing in front of this man, she couldn't ignore the truth.

He's right. She had thought she could escape her past, that this town could be the place where she could reinvent herself. But the memories, the habits, the way of thinking—it all lingered, just beneath the surface. No matter how much she tried to convince herself otherwise, she was still Sophia Bennett, the heiress to one of the wealthiest families in the country. And no amount of distance could erase that.

"You don't know anything about me," she shot back, her voice tinged with defensiveness. "You don't know what it's like to live in a world where everything is decided for you."

The man's eyes darkened, the amusement from earlier fading into something more intense, more dangerous. "I know more than you think," he said, his voice low and steady. "I know what it's like to have everything handed to you, to have every decision made for you by people who never cared about what you wanted. I know what it's like to be trapped in a life you didn't choose."

The words struck her like a lightning bolt. For the briefest moment, she saw a flicker of vulnerability in his eyes, something raw and human that he had been desperately trying to hide. But just as quickly, it was gone, replaced by the cold, unreadable mask he had worn from the start.

Sophia felt a shudder run through her, as though she had just glimpsed something she wasn't meant to see. There was more to this man than she had initially thought. And the more she tried to push him away, the more drawn to him she became.

He took another step closer, his eyes never leaving hers. "You're running, Sophia. But sooner or later, you're going to have to stop and face what you're really running from."

Her heart was pounding in her chest, her breath shallow as she stood frozen in place. She had thought she was escaping her past, but now it seemed as though it was chasing her. And this man—this mysterious stranger—knew it better than anyone else.

"Why are you doing this?" she whispered, barely able to keep her voice steady.

He didn't answer right away, his gaze softening just a fraction. "Because I see you," he said, his voice barely a breath. "I see the mask you wear, and I know the truth underneath."

The silence that followed was deafening, thick with the weight of his words, and for the first time in a long while, Sophia felt exposed, vulnerable in a way she had never known.

And just like that, everything shifted. What had started as an unsettling encounter now felt like the beginning of something far more dangerous—something that could unravel everything she had fought to leave behind.

Five

An Unlikely Friendship

The air was thick with tension, the silence between them almost unbearable. Sophia stood frozen, her gaze locked on the man before her. She hadn't expected this—hadn't expected to feel so exposed, so vulnerable in front of someone she barely knew. Her heart raced, each beat pounding in her ears as she tried to make sense of everything that had just happened.

She had come to this town seeking refuge, seeking the freedom to live without the weight of her family's expectations pressing down on her. But now, standing in front of this stranger—this man who seemed to know more about her than anyone else ever had—Sophia felt as though she were unraveling, piece by piece.

He had seen through her walls. He had pierced through the

layers of the life she had carefully constructed and exposed her fears, her insecurities, her guilt. And for the first time in a long time, she wasn't sure how to hide it all.

"I didn't ask for this," she said, her voice shaking slightly. She wasn't sure if she was speaking to him or to herself. "I didn't ask for this life. It wasn't my choice."

The man didn't respond immediately. His eyes were still fixed on her, his expression unreadable. He was studying her, as though he were trying to decipher something she couldn't even understand herself.

"I know," he said quietly, finally breaking the silence. "But it's the life you've been given. And you can't outrun it forever."

Sophia swallowed, the weight of his words settling in her chest. "I don't want to outrun it," she said, her voice low but firm. "I just want to be... free. Free from the expectations, from the constant pressure. I want to find out who I really am, without all the noise."

The man took a step back, his gaze never leaving hers. "And what do you think you'll find out there?" he asked, his tone tinged with a touch of skepticism. "What do you think is waiting for you in a life that doesn't have all that luxury, all that control?"

Sophia's breath hitched. He was right. She hadn't fully thought through what freedom actually meant. She had been so desperate to escape, so desperate to break away from everything she had known, that she hadn't considered what it would feel like to truly be free. Would she be happy? Would she find fulfillment in a life stripped of wealth and privilege?

She didn't have an answer.

"I don't know," she admitted, her voice quieter now. "I just know that I can't keep living like this. I can't keep pretending to be something I'm not. I've spent my whole life being someone else's idea of who I should be. I don't even recognize myself anymore."

The man nodded slowly, his eyes softening just a fraction. "I get it. I've been there too. I've lived a life where every decision was made for me, where I had no say in anything. And I hated it. But you can't just run away from it. You have to face it. You have to find a way to make peace with it."

Sophia looked at him, her mind swirling with questions. "How do you know all of this?" she asked. "How do you know what I've been through?"

His eyes flickered with something that resembled pain, but it was gone almost immediately. "Because I've been where you are. I was once just like you—caught in a world that didn't care about me, a world that only cared about what I could offer. And I hated it. But I realized something important along the way. You can't outrun who you are. You have to face it. You have to make a choice."

Sophia felt a pang of curiosity stir within her. She had known that there was something about him—something that had drawn her to him, something familiar. She had sensed it the moment they had locked eyes at the gala. But now, standing here in the darkened park with him, she realized there was more to this man than just his disdain for wealth and privilege. He had a story of his own. A story that was just as complicated as hers, if not more so.

"You don't have to share your story with me," she said softly, her voice a gentle invitation. "But if you want to, I'm listening."

For the first time since they had met, the man's expression shifted. It wasn't a smile, but it was something close—an acknowledgment, a crack in the armor he had built around himself. He seemed to hesitate, as though considering whether or not to speak. And then, without warning, he exhaled sharply, a sign of resignation.

"My name is Alex," he said, his voice low and guarded. "And I know what it's like to be trapped by your name, by your legacy. My family has money, too. More than I could ever need. But that's not what matters to them. It's about control. It's about power. They think that money can buy anything, even my soul."

Sophia's eyes widened slightly. She hadn't expected him to open up to her, not like this. His words struck a chord deep within her—so much of her own life had been shaped by her family's wealth, by their expectations of her. But Alex's words felt different. They felt like they came from a place of pain, of betrayal.

"I know what that's like," she whispered. "I know what it's like to feel like you're just a pawn in someone else's game."

Alex's eyes met hers, and for the first time, she saw a glimmer of understanding in them. "It's not just the money, though," he continued. "It's the power they think they have over you. The choices they try to make for you. My parents didn't care what I wanted. They didn't care about my happiness. They only cared about what I could do for them, for the family. So, I ran. I left everything behind."

Sophia's heart ached as she listened to his words. She didn't know what had driven him to run, but she could feel the weight of his past pressing down on him, just as it had pressed down on her for so long. She had been running too—running from a life that felt suffocating, a life that wasn't her own.

"But running didn't fix anything," Alex continued, his voice tinged with bitterness. "It didn't make the pain go away. It didn't make me feel free. It just made me more lost. I ended up here, in this damn town, thinking that somehow, I could escape it all. But it's not about escaping. It's about facing it. It's about understanding who you are, what you want, and what you're willing to fight for."

Sophia stared at him, her mind racing. He was right. Running hadn't fixed anything for her either. She had left everything behind in the hope of finding peace, but now, standing here with Alex, she realized that peace wouldn't come from hiding. It would come from confronting the past, from understanding her own worth beyond the money and the name.

"I don't know if I can do it," she said softly, her voice trembling slightly. "I don't know if I can face everything I've run from."

Alex looked at her, his expression softened. "You don't have to do it alone," he said quietly. "I know what it's like to feel like you're drowning in your own life. But you don't have to drown. Not anymore."

For a long moment, they stood in the quiet of the park, the weight of their shared understanding settling between them. It wasn't an easy path they had ahead of them, but in that moment, Sophia felt something shift inside her. She wasn't alone anymore. And maybe, just maybe, she could start to find her way.

"I'm not sure where this is going," Sophia said quietly, her voice barely above a whisper.

Alex gave her a small, almost imperceptible smile. "Neither am I. But we'll figure it out. Together."

And for the first time in a long time, Sophia felt like she wasn't running anymore. She was standing still, facing the future, whatever it might hold. With Alex by her side, she knew that maybe—just maybe—there was hope.

Six

Shared Secrets

The following days after her encounter with Alex felt like a blur to Sophia. It was as if a veil had been lifted, and the world she had left behind seemed far away, almost unreal. But the more she tried to settle into this new life, the more unsettled she felt. She hadn't expected the transition to be easy. After all, she had spent her entire life in a world of opulence, and now she was living in a small town where the air felt different, the people were different, and the expectations—well, they were nonexistent.

But it wasn't the town that unsettled her. It wasn't the small house she had chosen to call home, nor the simplicity of the life she was trying to build. It was Alex. His words, his presence, kept haunting her, like an echo she couldn't escape.

She couldn't deny the pull she felt toward him—the way he

seemed to understand her in a way no one else ever had. And the way he looked at her, as though he could see all the cracks in her carefully constructed façade, made her want to retreat into herself. He wasn't just a stranger; he was a mirror, reflecting the parts of herself she had tried to ignore for years.

Sophia sat on the porch of her house that evening, staring out at the quiet street. The sun was beginning to dip below the horizon, casting a soft, golden light across the town. She had been trying to keep busy, trying to avoid thinking too much about what she had left behind. But the emptiness inside her seemed to grow with each passing day, a gnawing hunger that she couldn't ignore.

The creak of the front gate startled her from her thoughts, and she looked up to see Alex walking toward her, his figure silhouetted against the fading light. Her heart skipped a beat, and for a moment, she felt like she couldn't breathe. She hadn't expected him to show up—hadn't expected him to seek her out again—but here he was, just as mysterious and enigmatic as ever.

He stopped a few feet from her, his eyes lingering on her for a moment before he spoke. "Mind if I join you?"

Sophia hesitated for a moment, unsure of what to say. She had told herself that she wouldn't get too close to him—that she couldn't afford to let anyone get too close—but here he was, standing in front of her, as though nothing had changed.

"Of course," she said, trying to sound casual as she gestured to the empty chair beside her. "I was just thinking."

Alex nodded and sat down next to her, his body language casual, but Sophia couldn't shake the feeling that there was something more beneath the surface. Something he wasn't saying. His silence was deafening, like an unspoken understanding between them, as though they both knew that neither one of them was truly free.

For a long moment, neither of them spoke. The sounds of the town, the rustling of the leaves in the trees, filled the space between them. It was a strange kind of peace, one that Sophia hadn't felt in years. But it was also suffocating. She couldn't shake the feeling that there was something unsaid, something important that needed to be addressed.

"So," she said, finally breaking the silence, her voice soft but steady, "what now?"

Alex didn't immediately respond, his gaze fixed on the horizon. The sun had almost completely disappeared, leaving only a sliver of light behind the mountains. He seemed to be lost in his thoughts, as though he were searching for the right words to say.

"I don't know," he said finally, his voice low and tinged with something that sounded almost like regret. "But I know we can't keep avoiding the truth. Not forever."

Sophia's heart skipped a beat. "What truth?" she asked, her voice barely above a whisper.

Alex turned to her then, his eyes dark with something unreadable. "The truth about who we are. About what we've left behind. About the things we've been running from."

Sophia's breath caught in her throat. She hadn't expected him to be so blunt, so open. She had expected him to deflect, to hide behind his walls, as he always had. But here he was, breaking down the very barriers she had built for herself.

"I'm not running anymore," she said, her voice shaky. She wasn't sure if she was talking to him or to herself. "I've come this far, and I don't want to keep hiding. But I don't know where to go from here."

Alex was quiet for a moment, as though he were considering her words carefully. He took a deep breath, then turned his full attention to her. "I don't have all the answers, Sophia," he said, his voice steady but raw. "But I think we can help each other figure it out."

Sophia looked at him, her heart pounding in her chest. His words made something stir inside her—a flicker of hope, maybe, or something more dangerous. She didn't know what it was, but it was enough to make her want to trust him. To take a leap of faith, even though she had no idea where it would lead.

"What do you mean?" she asked, her voice barely audible.

"I mean that we're both trapped in our own way," Alex said, his gaze intense. "We've both been running from the past, from the expectations, from everything that's been forced on us. But maybe it's time to stop running. Maybe it's time to face it head-on."

Sophia felt a tightness in her chest. The idea of facing everything she had left behind was terrifying. It was easier to keep running, easier to pretend that she could start over in this small town, where no one knew who she was. But Alex was right. She couldn't keep hiding. Sooner or later, she would have to confront her past, and it terrified her.

"I don't know if I can do that," she admitted, her voice barely above a whisper.

Alex's expression softened. "You don't have to do it alone," he said quietly. "We can figure it out together. It's not about forgetting your past—it's about understanding it. Owning it. Accepting it."

Sophia felt a knot in her stomach, but something else was growing inside her too. A sense of belonging. A sense of connection she hadn't felt in years. She didn't know if it was the right thing to do, or if Alex was simply offering her a lifeline because he didn't want to be alone in his own struggles, but in that moment, it didn't matter. She had spent so long hiding from the truth, running from the life she had been born into. But now, with Alex beside her, she felt like maybe—just maybe—she could face it.

"Okay," she said, her voice firm now. "I'll try."

Alex nodded, his gaze softening as he gave her a small, almost imperceptible smile. "That's all I'm asking."

They sat in silence for a long moment, the air between them thick with unspoken understanding. The night had fallen completely now, and the stars above them seemed to shine brighter than ever before. It was a moment of peace, a fleeting moment in time where they were simply two people, sitting together in the quiet of the world, knowing that everything was about to change.

Sophia didn't know what the future held, or what steps she would have to take to confront her past. But for the first time in a long time, she felt like she wasn't alone in it. With Alex beside her, maybe, just maybe, she could face the secrets that had been haunting her for so long.

And as the night deepened around them, Sophia couldn't shake the feeling that this was the beginning of something far more complicated—and far more dangerous—than she had ever imagined.

Seven

A Glimpse Into His World

The next few weeks passed in a blur of uncertainty and quiet revelations. Sophia had made a choice: to stay, to face her past and the life she had once known. But each day brought new challenges, new questions that she wasn't sure how to answer. The town had started to feel more like home—small, quiet, and free of the constant pressure she had faced in the city. But the sense of freedom wasn't as comforting as she'd hoped. The truth was, she was still running in her mind. She was still hiding from the life she had left behind. And the hardest part was facing the fact that she didn't know who she was without that world, without the wealth, the legacy, the expectations.

And then there was Alex.

It was hard to explain what was happening between them. He

wasn't like anyone she had ever known. His presence in her life was like a riddle, one that she couldn't quite solve. He had his own demons—his own past, one he had barely spoken of. But it didn't stop him from becoming the one person she could talk to, the one person who understood what it was like to feel trapped by your own circumstances. Their connection was like a thread between two broken pieces, holding them together even as they tried to figure out who they were outside of their pasts.

The sound of footsteps on the gravel path outside the house snapped Sophia out of her thoughts. She had been sitting on the porch, watching the world go by, her mind lost in the uncertainty of her future. The sun was starting to set, casting long shadows across the street. She knew who it was before she even turned around. It was always him. He seemed to appear out of nowhere, like a shadow she couldn't escape.

Alex stepped onto the porch, his usual quiet demeanor more apparent than ever. His eyes scanned her for a moment, as though measuring her—assessing something. Sophia stood up, brushing off her jeans as she looked at him. His presence had become almost as familiar as the town itself, yet it always carried a weight that left her wondering where it was leading.

"You're out here again," he said, his voice low, but his eyes searching. "Why do you always sit out here, alone?"

Sophia shrugged, trying to play it off like it wasn't something that affected her. "I like the quiet. It gives me time to think. Time to breathe."

A Glimpse Into His World

Alex nodded slowly, as if he understood exactly what she meant. There were times when the quiet felt like a balm for the wounds she'd carried for so long, and other times it felt like it was suffocating her, drowning her in thoughts she wasn't ready to face.

She stepped back and gestured for him to sit down. "Do you want to stay for a while?" she asked. "We can talk, or not talk. Whatever you need."

Alex paused, his gaze flickering to the empty chair beside her, then back to her face. His expression seemed unreadable, like he was always carrying a weight of his own. But the vulnerability in his eyes betrayed him. For a moment, he looked like he wanted to say something, but then he seemed to push it back, bury it deep. He sat down, his posture rigid, as though even here, on this quiet porch, he was still carrying the burden of something he hadn't shared.

Sophia didn't ask about it. Not yet. She knew that pressing him would only make him close off further. Instead, she leaned back in her chair, her gaze falling on the horizon. The air was thick with the scent of earth and pine, the calm before nightfall. It was one of those rare moments when everything felt still, when time seemed to slow just enough for her to catch her breath.

"You know, I've been thinking a lot lately," she said, her voice soft, almost hesitant. "About how I've been running for so long. I thought coming here would fix everything. I thought it would be the escape I needed."

Alex didn't say anything for a while, letting her words settle in the air between them. Then, his voice came, low and measured. "You can't outrun your past, Sophia. Not forever. You can't keep pretending it's not there. It's a part of you, just like the rest of who you are."

Sophia looked at him, her heart tightening at the weight of his words. "I don't want to be a part of it anymore. I don't want to live in the shadow of my family's expectations, or live a life that was chosen for me."

"I know," Alex said, his eyes steady on hers. "But it's not that simple. You can't just choose to forget what you are. The world doesn't work like that."

Sophia clenched her fists in her lap, frustration bubbling up. She had tried to ignore the truth for so long, telling herself that the fresh start in this small town would be enough to wash away everything that came before it. But deep down, she knew he was right. It wasn't that simple. She couldn't just pretend to be someone else. She had to face what she had been running from.

"I'm not sure I can do this," she admitted, her voice barely above a whisper. "I don't know who I am without everything I've been taught to be."

Alex's gaze softened. "You'll figure it out," he said quietly. "It's not about becoming someone else. It's about rediscovering who you are beneath all the layers they forced on you. It's about accepting what you can't change, and learning to live with it."

A Glimpse Into His World

Sophia swallowed hard, his words sinking deep into her. She wasn't sure what she was looking for—what he was offering her—but in that moment, she felt a stirring of something inside her. Maybe it was hope. Maybe it was the promise of something more. But whatever it was, she knew that this was a turning point. She couldn't keep running from herself. She couldn't keep hiding behind the past.

The sound of the wind rustling through the trees filled the silence between them, and for a moment, neither of them spoke. But in that silence, something shifted. Sophia could feel it. It was the fragile bond between them, the unspoken understanding that had grown over the past few weeks. She didn't know where it would lead, but she knew she couldn't turn back.

"You said you were running, too," she said suddenly, her voice trembling slightly. "From what?"

Alex stiffened for just a moment, his jaw tightening. But he didn't look away. Instead, he let out a deep breath, as though preparing himself for something. "It's complicated," he said slowly, his voice rough. "My family wasn't like yours. They didn't have wealth or power. But they had expectations, just the same. They had a vision for who I was supposed to be. And when I didn't fit into that vision, they made it clear I was a failure. A disappointment."

Sophia could hear the bitterness in his voice, the deep-seated anger that still lingered beneath the surface. But there was something else there too. Pain. Regret. A desire to be understood.

"What happened?" she asked, her voice soft with curiosity, but also something deeper—something that made her want to reach out to him. She didn't know what it was, but it was there, a connection she couldn't ignore.

Alex hesitated, his eyes clouded with memories he wasn't ready to share. "I left," he said finally, his voice hardening. "I couldn't be who they wanted me to be. So I left. And I've been running ever since. But sometimes, it feels like I'm still trapped. Like I'm carrying their expectations with me, even if they're not physically there."

Sophia nodded slowly, the weight of his words sinking in. She understood that feeling. She knew what it was like to live under the pressure of someone else's expectations. To feel like you were never enough, no matter how hard you tried.

"I'm sorry," she said, her voice quiet, sincere.

Alex looked at her then, his gaze softening for just a moment. "It's not your fault," he said, his voice low. "But sometimes, I wish I could stop running. Stop pretending."

Sophia felt her heart ache for him. She had been running too. From her past, from the life she had been born into. But Alex had been running for so much longer. And somehow, they had both ended up here, in this small town, facing the same truths they had spent so long avoiding.

A Glimpse Into His World

"What now?" she asked, her voice tentative, unsure.

Alex looked at her for a long time, as though considering her question carefully. "Now," he said softly, "we stop running. We face the fragments of our past, and we start putting them together. Piece by piece."

Sophia took a deep breath, her heart pounding in her chest. She didn't know what the future held. But in that moment, she knew one thing for sure: the fragmented pieces of her world could be mended. And maybe, just maybe, Alex would be there to help her put them back together.

Eight

The Reveal

Sophia spent the next few days trying to silence the echo of Alex's words in her mind, but it wasn't working. She kept thinking about his promise—about how they were going to face the fragments of their pasts, piece by piece. But something gnawed at her, a quiet fear that she couldn't shake. What if those pieces didn't fit together? What if, after all this time of running, all that was left was a pile of brokenness?

She had never realized how deeply her past had rooted itself in her. It had been easier to ignore it, to shove it into a corner of her mind and lock the door. But Alex had forced it to the surface, had dragged her into the painful reality of who she was. Who she had been. And now, every step forward felt like a risk. What if she didn't like what she found?

Sophia was standing in front of her kitchen window one

The Reveal

morning when the answer came crashing into her thoughts.

It was one of those quiet mornings—nothing stirring but the birds in the trees and the faint rustle of the leaves. The stillness felt like a breath held in time. She leaned against the counter, looking out at the town, lost in her thoughts. The sun was still low in the sky, casting long shadows across the empty street.

This is it, she thought. The moment when everything changes.

She had been avoiding it—avoiding looking too closely at the life she had left behind. But there it was, waiting for her, just beneath the surface. The science. The research. The obsession.

Her fingers tightened around the mug of tea she was holding, the heat seeping into her palms. She could feel it again, the old urge. The need to dissect, to analyze, to break things apart until they made sense. It was a part of her, something that had always driven her when nothing else could. It had been the only thing she had ever been truly good at—the only thing that made her feel like she was in control.

But it was also the one thing that had destroyed everything.

Sophia set the mug down with a soft clink, feeling the weight of her decision pressing down on her. She had been running from the world of science, from her father's expectations of her as a brilliant scientist, a future leader in the prestigious family business. She had been avoiding the legacy he had tried to impose on her. But it was never something she could just escape. It was a part of her—an obsession she couldn't outrun.

Her father had always believed in the power of knowledge, in the ability of science to change the world. But to him, it was never about finding answers. It was about control. About using knowledge as a tool to manipulate, to assert power over people. He had pushed her relentlessly, demanding excellence, demanding results, until she had broken under the pressure.

Sophia closed her eyes, remembering the countless nights spent in laboratories, her hands shaking with exhaustion, her mind overrun with formulas and theories, her father's voice always in the background, telling her that she could do better, be better. There was no escape from his voice, no escape from his expectations.

And then there was the project—the one that had ultimately broken her. The one that had driven her to flee, to abandon everything she had worked for.

It was meant to be revolutionary. A breakthrough in the field of environmental science. A project that promised to change the world, to solve some of the planet's most pressing problems. But it had all gone wrong. Her research, her findings, had been twisted, manipulated. The results were compromised. She had uncovered something she shouldn't have, and in the end, it had cost her more than just her reputation.

Sophia's stomach churned at the memory. The day she had realized what had happened was the day her world had fallen apart. The day she had learned the truth about her father's business, about the lengths they would go to protect their image, to hide the flaws in their perfect world. The day she had finally

The Reveal

broken free.

But now, as she stood in this small house, in this quiet town, the weight of it all had come rushing back. She had thought she could start fresh. But she had never truly left. The obsession with perfection, with answers, with control—it was still a part of her.

The sound of a knock on the door startled her from her thoughts. She jumped, her heart pounding as she walked toward the door. She wasn't expecting anyone. Not at this hour. She opened it slowly, her mind still tangled in the web of her past.

It was Alex.

He was standing on the doorstep, his expression unreadable, his posture tense. There was something different about him today—something that made her feel a flicker of anxiety deep in her chest.

"Hey," she said, trying to keep her voice steady, though she could feel the unease bubbling under the surface. "Is everything okay?"

Alex nodded, his gaze flickering to the side before he met her eyes again. "Can I come in?"

Sophia stepped aside without saying anything, her mind racing. There was something in his eyes, a kind of urgency, something that didn't belong here. She led him to the living room, where they both sat in silence for a moment, the air thick with unspoken tension.

"What's going on?" she asked finally, her voice barely above a whisper.

Alex ran a hand through his hair, his eyes clouded with something—something she couldn't quite place. He took a deep breath, and for a moment, it seemed like he wasn't sure whether or not to speak. But then, he did.

"I found something," he said, his voice low, almost cautious. "Something that I think you need to see."

Sophia's heart skipped a beat. "What are you talking about?"

Alex hesitated again, then reached into his jacket pocket and pulled out a folder. He set it on the coffee table in front of them, pushing it toward her.

She stared at the folder, unsure of what it contained. There was something about the way he was acting—something that made her feel like this wasn't just another casual conversation. This was important. This mattered.

Without thinking, she reached for the folder, her hands trembling slightly as she opened it. Inside were several pages of printed text, along with a few photographs. Sophia's breath caught in her throat as she scanned the pages. It was all there—the research, the project, the data she had left behind.

She looked up at Alex, her heart pounding. "How did you get

The Reveal

this?"

He didn't answer right away, his eyes avoiding hers. "I've been doing some digging," he said after a moment. "I knew there was something you weren't telling me. Something important. And I think I found it."

Sophia's mind raced as she processed the information in front of her. It was her work—her research. The project she had abandoned. But it wasn't just her findings that were in this folder. There were more details—details she hadn't known, or had chosen to ignore. There was a piece of the puzzle she hadn't seen before, something that threatened to unravel everything.

"The data's been manipulated," she whispered, her voice shaking with the weight of the realization. "They've covered it up. They've been hiding the truth."

Alex nodded slowly, his eyes never leaving hers. "I think you were right all along, Sophia. They used your work for their own agenda. But now it's coming back to haunt them."

Her hands shook as she set the folder down, trying to steady her breath. Her mind was racing, the pieces of the puzzle clicking together. Her father's company, the research, the project—it had all been a carefully constructed lie. She had known that it wasn't right. She had known that something was off. But this… this was worse than she had imagined.

"You have to help me," she said suddenly, the words tumbling out before she could stop them. "I have to stop this. I have to expose them."

Alex's gaze hardened, his jaw clenching. "It's not going to be easy, Sophia. They won't let you get away with it. They'll come after you. They'll do everything in their power to silence you."

Sophia's heart pounded in her chest. She had never felt more terrified in her life. But she knew one thing for sure—she couldn't run anymore. The pieces of her life had already been shattered, and now it was time to put them back together. But this time, she wouldn't be doing it alone.

"I'm not running anymore," she said, her voice steady with resolve. "I'm going to finish what I started. And this time, I'm going to make sure the truth is heard."

As Alex looked at her, there was something in his eyes—something she couldn't name. It was a mixture of fear and determination, of understanding and hope. And in that moment, she knew. Whatever came next, they would face it together.

The game had changed. And Sophia was ready to play.

Nine

Confrontation

The wind howled through the trees, the chill of the night creeping through the cracks in the walls of Sophia's house. It was the kind of night that pressed against your skin, urging you to stay indoors, to lock the doors and forget the world outside. But Sophia couldn't stay still, couldn't hide away from what she knew had to come next. She couldn't escape it anymore—not the past, not the truth.

The folder Alex had given her still lay open on the table in front of her. The contents of it were enough to make her blood run cold. The data, the research, the photographs—they were all evidence of the manipulation, of the betrayal that had come from the people she had trusted the most. Her father's company, the business she had once thought was the pinnacle of scientific progress, was nothing more than a façade—a machine built on lies, on secrecy, and on the exploitation of people's trust.

Sophia paced back and forth across the room, the floor creaking beneath her as she tried to make sense of everything. Her mind was swirling with the possibilities, the questions that had been building for months. What had she uncovered? What did this mean for her? For the people involved?

The sound of a knock at the door made her freeze mid-step. It was a quiet sound, but it carried the weight of something unknown, something urgent. She hadn't expected anyone, not this late. Not with everything that had been happening.

Her heart pounded in her chest as she crossed the room, her footsteps echoing in the silence. She reached for the doorknob, her fingers trembling slightly, and pulled it open.

Standing in front of her was Alex. His expression was tight, his eyes dark with something she couldn't quite place.

"What is it?" she asked, her voice a mix of concern and apprehension. "What's wrong?"

Alex didn't answer right away. He was breathing heavily, his gaze flickering nervously around the yard as if checking for something—or someone. There was a look in his eyes that made Sophia's stomach churn, a look that spoke of something more dangerous than anything she had faced so far.

"I need you to listen to me," Alex said, his voice low and strained. "We don't have much time. They're coming."

Sophia felt a cold rush of dread surge through her veins. She

Confrontation

knew exactly what he meant. The company. Her father. The people who had used her, manipulated her—they were coming for her, and they wouldn't stop until they had silenced her, until they had buried the truth.

"Who? Who's coming?" she asked, trying to steady her breath.

"Your father's people," Alex replied, his voice urgent. "They know what you're trying to do. They've been watching you. They're onto us."

Sophia's heart raced, and she felt the walls closing in. She had suspected that something like this might happen—that her decision to go public with the information, to expose the truth, would not go unnoticed. But she had underestimated the lengths her father's company would go to protect itself. She had underestimated how far they would be willing to reach to silence the one person who could destroy everything they had built.

"Do they know where I am?" she asked, her voice barely a whisper.

"I don't know," Alex said, his gaze flickering to the street, to the shadows that lingered just outside. "But we can't take any chances. We have to move quickly. You need to get out of here. Now."

Sophia stood frozen for a moment, the weight of the decision pressing down on her. Everything in her wanted to resist, to stay, to confront the people who had destroyed everything she had worked for. But she knew Alex was right. She wasn't safe here. And if they were as close as Alex suggested, there was no time to waste.

"What do we do?" she asked, her voice barely audible.

Alex took a deep breath, his eyes never leaving the road behind him. "I've been making arrangements. We can't go to the authorities—they're too connected. But I have a place. A safe place where we can lay low until we figure out our next move."

Sophia felt a surge of panic rise in her chest. "Safe place? What do you mean? I don't know if I can trust anyone anymore, Alex. Not after everything."

He turned to face her, his expression softening. "I understand. But you don't have a choice right now. You can't stay here. Not with them looking for you."

She wanted to argue, wanted to push back against the idea of running, of hiding. But the truth was, she didn't have a choice. She was already in too deep, and if she stayed, she would be risking everything. Her life. Her future. Her very identity.

"Okay," she said quietly, the words catching in her throat. "I'll go. But you have to promise me one thing, Alex."

"What?" he asked, his brow furrowing in confusion.

"Promise me that we'll find a way to finish this. To expose the truth. We can't let them get away with it."

Confrontation

Alex's expression softened, and he gave her a nod. "I promise."

Sophia grabbed her jacket from the back of the chair, her hands shaking as she slipped it on. She grabbed the folder from the table and tucked it into her bag, the weight of it like a reminder of everything she was about to leave behind.

"I'll be right behind you," Alex said, stepping back toward the door, his eyes scanning the yard once more.

They moved quickly, slipping out the back door and into the shadows of the night. The streets were eerily quiet, the silence pressing in on them like a heavy weight. Every noise seemed to be amplified—the soft crunch of their footsteps on the gravel, the faint rustle of the wind through the trees. It felt like the calm before the storm.

Sophia's heart was pounding in her chest, her mind racing with thoughts of what would come next. Where would they go? What would they do? Would they even be safe, or were they walking straight into a trap?

Alex led the way, his footsteps steady, his eyes sharp and alert. They reached the edge of town, where the streets grew darker and the houses became fewer and farther apart. The air was cooler here, the smell of pine and damp earth thick in the air. They moved swiftly, crossing a small bridge that led into the outskirts of town, where a narrow dirt road wound its way toward the woods.

It wasn't much farther now, Alex said. The safe place he

had spoken of—his refuge—was just beyond the trees. It was isolated, hidden away from prying eyes. But even as they drew closer to their destination, Sophia couldn't shake the feeling that they weren't alone.

A sudden rustle in the trees sent a chill down her spine. She froze, her breath caught in her throat. Alex's hand shot out, grabbing her arm and pulling her into the shadows. They pressed against the trunk of a tree, their bodies still, their breaths shallow.

Sophia's heart pounded in her chest as she strained to hear, her ears ringing with the sounds of the night. Was it just the wind? Or was someone out there, watching them?

"I don't think we're alone," Alex whispered, his voice barely audible.

Sophia nodded, her mind racing. She could hear footsteps now, faint but unmistakable. Someone was out there. Someone was following them.

Alex pulled her closer, his grip tightening around her wrist. "We need to move, now," he said, his voice urgent.

They turned and sprinted down the dirt road, the sounds of pursuit growing closer with each passing second. Sophia's breath was coming in short gasps, the weight of the situation crashing down on her. Whoever was behind them wasn't just following—they were hunting. And they weren't going to stop until they had found them.

Confrontation

The trees seemed to close in around them, the shadows growing darker with each step they took. They were running blind now, their path uncertain, but there was no turning back. They had to keep moving. They had to keep fighting.

The sound of footsteps grew louder, and Sophia risked a glance over her shoulder. Her eyes locked onto a figure emerging from the trees, silhouetted against the dim light. It was too late to outrun them. Too late to hide.

And in that moment, she knew—this wasn't just about exposing the truth. This was about survival. The game had changed, and she was in it for good.

"Run!" Alex shouted, his voice sharp with panic. "Run, Sophia!"

Sophia didn't need any more encouragement. She turned and ran, her heart hammering in her chest, her mind racing with thoughts of what would come next. Would they make it? Would they survive long enough to expose the truth? Would they ever be free?

The darkness closed in around them as they ran, but there was no turning back now. They were fighting for everything—everything they had lost, and everything they were about to risk.

Ten

A Difficult Decision

Sophia's breath came in ragged gasps as she ran, her feet pounding against the dirt road. The sound of footsteps behind her was too close—too real—too threatening. She could hear the heavy crunch of boots on the gravel, the sound of pursuit that seemed to grow louder with every passing second. Panic surged through her veins as her mind raced, trying to think, to calculate, to find a way out.

Alex was a few steps ahead, his strides long and purposeful, his eyes scanning the path ahead with a look of determination that matched the urgency in her own chest. The trees on either side of the road loomed like dark sentinels, their branches twisting like the hands of unseen figures, reaching out to pull her back into the nightmare she had been running from for so long.

She could feel the weight of the situation crashing down on her.

A Difficult Decision

They were being hunted, and the only thing standing between them and whatever dark fate awaited them was the thin thread of hope that they might find refuge in time. But the woods seemed endless, the road winding through them in a maze of uncertainty.

Why had she thought this would work? she thought desperately, pushing her body harder. Why had she thought she could outrun them?

Her legs screamed in protest, her lungs burning from the effort, but she forced herself to keep going, to keep putting one foot in front of the other. She wasn't sure how long they had been running, but the night had grown colder, the shadows deeper. There were no signs of life, no lights from houses or cars, just the eerie stillness of the forest surrounding them.

And then, just as she thought she couldn't run any longer, she heard it—a sudden, sharp crack in the underbrush. She turned her head, her heart pounding even harder. The figure that had been chasing them emerged from the trees, a silhouette against the faint moonlight. It was a man, tall and broad-shouldered, his face obscured by the darkness, but the unmistakable glint of a flashlight in his hand was enough to confirm what she feared.

Alex stopped dead in his tracks, his body tensing as he turned toward the figure. There was no hesitation in his movements as he stepped forward, positioning himself between Sophia and the man, a protective instinct she had come to recognize in him.

"Stay behind me," Alex whispered, his voice low but firm.

Sophia's eyes darted between Alex and the man, her mind racing for a way out. But before she could move, the man stepped forward, his voice cutting through the silence like a blade.

"You're not going anywhere," the man said, his voice gravelly and cold. "This ends tonight."

Sophia's pulse shot into her throat, her eyes wide with fear. They knew. They knew everything.

Alex's gaze hardened, his jaw clenched with determination. "We're not going back," he said, his voice unwavering. "Not now. Not ever."

The man laughed, but it was a dry, humorless sound. "You think you can run forever? You've already seen too much. You've already made your choice."

Sophia could feel the tension in the air, the oppressive weight of the moment pressing down on them. They were outnumbered, outmatched, and they had nowhere to go. The woods were thick with shadows, and the man's words echoed in her mind, growing louder with every beat of her heart. They had crossed a line—one that couldn't be undone.

"We don't have to do this," Alex said, his voice calm but laced with a quiet fury. "You don't have to follow through with whatever plan you think you're executing. There's still time to fix this."

The man's eyes gleamed in the darkness. "It's too late for that.

A Difficult Decision

You should've known better than to play this game. Now, you'll pay the price."

Sophia's breath caught in her throat, her fingers tightening around the strap of her bag. This wasn't a game. Not anymore. This was real. This was life and death.

Before she could react, Alex lunged forward, his movements swift and deliberate. In a flash, the man was on the ground, the flashlight rolling away into the darkened woods. The fight was over as quickly as it had begun, and Alex stood over the man, his chest heaving with exertion, his expression hard and cold.

"Is he alive?" Sophia whispered, her voice shaky as she stepped forward, still unsure whether to believe what had just happened.

Alex glanced down at the man, his eyes narrowing. "For now. But we don't have time to waste. We have to keep moving."

Sophia nodded, her heart still hammering in her chest. She couldn't let her guard down. Not now. She wasn't sure if it was the fear, the adrenaline, or the sheer exhaustion from running that made everything feel like a blur. But she had learned one thing in these moments: they were in danger. There was no escaping it, no running from it. They were in too deep.

She forced herself to turn away from the man on the ground and focus on the road ahead. She didn't know where it would lead them, but she couldn't stop now. She had no choice but to follow Alex, to trust that he knew what he was doing.

They pushed forward, the tension between them palpable, the sound of their footsteps the only thing keeping them grounded. Sophia's thoughts raced as they navigated the darkened path, trying to make sense of everything. She couldn't stop thinking about her father's company, about the lives that had been destroyed because of their greed and lies. She couldn't stop thinking about the promises Alex had made—the promises to expose the truth, to bring everything to light.

But the truth wasn't as simple as she had imagined. It wasn't as clean as she had hoped. And now, as they ran through the forest, she knew—there was no going back.

They reached the clearing at the edge of the woods, and Sophia felt a strange sense of relief. They were out of the trees, out of the suffocating darkness. The moonlight bathed the field in an eerie glow, casting long shadows across the ground.

And then, in the stillness of the night, it happened.

Alex turned toward her, his expression softer now, more vulnerable. There was something in his eyes—something that had been building between them for weeks, something that neither of them had been willing to acknowledge until now.

For a moment, everything seemed to stop. The world fell away, and it was just the two of them, standing in the moonlight, their breath coming in shallow gasps.

Sophia felt her heart race as Alex took a step toward her. The air between them crackled with a strange intensity, and before

A Difficult Decision

she could say anything, Alex was there, his hand reaching out to her, his fingers brushing against her cheek.

His touch sent a shockwave through her, and without thinking, she closed the distance between them. Their lips met in a kiss that was urgent, desperate, as though they were both trying to hold onto something they had been afraid to admit—something they had been running from.

The kiss was everything. It was passion, fear, hope. It was the weight of their shared past and the uncertainty of their future. It was the kiss that shouldn't have happened, the kiss that defied every reason to hold back.

When they pulled apart, the silence that followed was deafening. Sophia's chest was tight, her breath shallow. She couldn't look at him. Not yet. The kiss had been too much, too raw. And for the first time in her life, she felt both vulnerable and alive.

But the moment passed quickly, as everything did in their world. There was no time for lingering. No time for emotions to settle. They had crossed a line they couldn't un-cross, and the consequences of their actions were already rushing toward them, faster than they could outrun.

Sophia took a step back, her eyes still not meeting his. "We need to keep moving," she said, her voice barely above a whisper.

Alex nodded, his expression unreadable. "Yeah. We do."

And so, they ran again—together, but with the weight of

everything that had just happened between them. The kiss had changed something, something that neither of them was ready to face. But for now, there was no turning back.

Eleven

Breaking the Walls

Sophia's heart raced as she and Alex hurried through the dense woods, their feet crunching against the dry underbrush. The sudden kiss had left a tremor in her chest, one that refused to subside no matter how fast they ran or how hard she tried to shake it off. Every step felt like it brought them closer to something they weren't prepared for, something she wasn't sure she even wanted. It wasn't just the fear of being caught—of the unknown dangers that might be lurking in the dark—it was the inexplicable tension that had crept into their relationship.

The world had changed in that brief moment. The kiss had broken something open, something that had been buried beneath their shared trauma, their secrets, and their survival instincts. She wasn't sure if it was the danger they were in or something else entirely, but the bond between them had shifted, and it felt like they were no longer just two people running from the same past. Now, they were something more—something neither of them had planned for.

"Do you think we've lost them?" she whispered, her voice strained as they slowed to a walk, still scanning the forest around them. The adrenaline from their flight was starting to fade, leaving her with a sense of vulnerability she wasn't used to.

Alex didn't answer right away. His eyes were fixed on the path ahead, and Sophia noticed the tightness in his jaw, the way his hands clenched at his sides as if trying to keep his composure intact. He was always composed, always in control. But tonight—tonight, something had changed in him too.

"I don't know," he finally replied, his voice low, guarded. "But we have to keep moving. We can't risk staying in one place for too long."

Sophia nodded, her pulse still racing. She understood the urgency. They had crossed a line, and now, there was no turning back. The company's enforcers were closing in, and they wouldn't stop until they had silenced her, until they had erased any trace of the truth she had uncovered.

Her eyes darted around the woods, trying to find something familiar, something that could give her a sense of safety. The darkness was suffocating, the shadows pressing in on them from all sides. The trees around them towered like silent sentinels, their branches twisted and gnarled, their leaves

Breaking the Walls

rustling in the wind.

As they pressed forward, the faint glint of light caught her eye, a soft glow that seemed to pulse from somewhere up ahead. Sophia squinted into the distance, her heart fluttering with a mix of hope and suspicion. Could it be a sign of help? A safe haven? Or was it another trap?

"Alex," she whispered urgently, tugging at his sleeve. "Do you see that?"

He stopped in his tracks, his eyes narrowing as he scanned the direction she was pointing. For a moment, his face was unreadable, but then he nodded. "I see it."

They made their way toward the light cautiously, their footsteps barely audible in the dense underbrush. The closer they got, the more the air seemed to hum with a strange energy. The light was faint, but it was there—a soft, ethereal glow that seemed to pulse with life.

As they approached the source of the light, Sophia's breath caught in her throat. Before her stood a small, unassuming cabin—weathered and old, but with a faint glow emanating from the windows. The light wasn't from a lamp or any visible source; it seemed to come from within the walls themselves, as though the very structure of the cabin was alive with some hidden energy.

Sophia's mind raced as they stood there in silence, trying to make sense of what they were seeing. She had never heard of this place before, but Alex seemed to recognize it. He was staring at the cabin with an expression she couldn't read—somewhere between awe and fear.

"This is it," Alex murmured, almost to himself. "The place I told you about."

Sophia's brow furrowed. "The safe place? What is this? What's going on here?"

Alex turned to her, his eyes intense. "It's not just a place. It's something… more. Something you won't understand unless you're willing to trust me."

She didn't answer immediately, her mind racing with questions. Was this really a safe haven, or was it another trap? But the desperation in Alex's eyes made her hesitate. She had no choice but to follow him, to trust him—at least for now. They had come too far, and there was nowhere else to go.

Alex pushed open the door, the creaking sound echoing in the stillness of the night. The cabin was small but comfortable, its interior dimly lit by the same strange glow that had surrounded the outside. The air inside felt thick, charged with a strange energy that made the hairs on the back of Sophia's neck stand on end. There was something about this place that felt… different.

"Where are we?" Sophia asked again, her voice tinged with uncertainty. "What is this place, Alex?"

Alex stepped further into the cabin, his gaze fixed on something

Breaking the Walls

in the far corner. There was an old wooden table, scattered with papers, maps, and strange mechanical devices that looked like they belonged in a lab. Sophia's eyes widened as she took in the sight. This wasn't just a cabin. It was something else—something hidden, something secret.

"This," Alex said, turning back to her, "is where it all began. This is the place where we discovered the truth."

Sophia's heart skipped a beat. The truth. The very thing she had been chasing, the thing that had led her to this moment, was right here in front of her. But she didn't understand. What did Alex mean? How did this place tie into everything?

Alex moved toward the table, his fingers brushing across the maps. "You see," he continued, "the research we were doing—it wasn't just about environmental science. It was about something bigger. Something your father's company didn't want anyone to know. They've been hiding the truth for years. And this cabin… it's where we first started to uncover it."

Sophia's mind was spinning. She had heard rumors of secret research, of things her father's company had done in the shadows, but she had never known the full extent of it. Her own involvement in the project had been limited to her father's expectations—always focused on the science, never the ethics. She had never realized how far the corruption ran until now.

"What is it?" she whispered, her voice trembling. "What's the truth?"

Alex turned to face her, his expression serious. "It's not just about pollution or climate change. It's about manipulating the very fabric of reality itself."

Sophia's breath caught in her throat. "What do you mean? How could—how could they—"

Alex's eyes met hers, and for the first time, Sophia saw a flicker of something darker in his gaze. "They've been experimenting with time, Sophia. With parallel dimensions. With the very laws of nature. They've found a way to manipulate time—to alter the flow of events. And your father, he was at the center of it all."

The words hung in the air between them, thick with disbelief. Sophia's mind struggled to make sense of what Alex was saying. Time manipulation? Parallel dimensions? It sounded impossible—like something out of a science fiction novel. But the look in Alex's eyes told her it was all too real.

Her heart pounded in her chest as she stepped closer to the table, her eyes scanning the papers and devices. There were equations, formulas, notes in her father's handwriting, all talking about something—some experiment that bridged the gap between two worlds. Sophia felt a cold chill wash over her as she realized what this meant. Her father's company hadn't just been hiding the truth about the environment. They had been playing with forces they couldn't control—forces that could tear apart the very fabric of time itself.

"This is bigger than anything I thought," Sophia whispered, her voice shaking.

Alex stepped closer, his expression hardening. "And it's not over. They're still working on it. They've already opened the rift. And they'll stop at nothing to cover up what they've done."

Sophia's head spun. She had thought she was running from corporate corruption, from a company that was willing to sacrifice anything for profit. But this—this was something far more dangerous. This was about power, manipulation, and something that could change the course of history. And she had no idea how deep the rabbit hole went.

"We need to stop them," she said, her voice firm now, as the weight of their mission settled in. "We need to expose them before they destroy everything."

Alex nodded grimly. "And we will. But we have to be careful. The rift—they're using it to do things. Things they shouldn't be doing."

Sophia's mind raced as she tried to piece everything together. The rift. The parallel worlds. It was all connected. And she had just stepped into something far bigger than she could have imagined.

"Then let's do it," she said, her voice steady now, determination replacing the fear that had once gripped her. "Let's fix this."

Twelve

The Tipping Point

The cabin felt like a sanctuary and a prison all at once. The warmth inside was in stark contrast to the cold night outside, but the flickering light from the fireplace only seemed to highlight the tension that hung thick in the air. Sophia's mind raced as she pored over the papers scattered across the table, trying to piece together the fragments of information she had just learned. Time manipulation. Parallel dimensions. Her father's role in it all. None of it made sense, and yet, it all felt so overwhelmingly real.

Alex was pacing in the corner, his hands clenched into fists as if trying to wrangle the storm inside him. His eyes flicked over the papers occasionally, but he seemed more preoccupied with his own thoughts than the research in front of them.

"You're thinking too much," Sophia said suddenly, her voice

The Tipping Point

breaking the silence. She looked up from the table, meeting his gaze. "We need to focus on what's next. We can't just sit here and wait for them to come after us."

Alex froze mid-step, his gaze sharpening. "You think I'm not aware of that?" His tone was low, clipped. "But we can't just charge in blindly, Sophia. This is bigger than anything we've ever faced. You saw the data. Your father's research isn't just about manipulating time; it's about tearing through realities themselves. If we don't move carefully, we might be walking straight into a trap."

Sophia stood, her heart pounding in her chest. She wasn't afraid of the danger—she had already faced that. What terrified her now was the realization that her father had known about the rift for years. He had opened it, and now it threatened to unravel everything. The company, the experiments, the strange power they had found—it was all connected. And she wasn't sure who she could trust anymore.

Her eyes flicked to the papers again, taking in the equations and diagrams, the technical jargon that seemed to make her head spin. But there was one thing that stood out above everything else: the rift. Her father's notes detailed how they had manipulated it to gain access to other dimensions, and that wasn't all. There were references to "watchers," strange entities that observed the rift, entities whose purpose remained unclear but whose presence felt like a warning.

"What are these?" Sophia whispered, pointing at a set of notes she hadn't yet examined. They were scrawled in her father's precise handwriting but felt alien in their content—filled with cryptic mentions of "rifts in the fabric," "distorted timelines," and, most disturbingly, "the watchers."

Alex moved over to the table, his gaze scanning the notes. He bent closer, his jaw tightening. "I don't know," he said quietly. "But I've seen these before. Not in your father's work, but in the files I've been tracking. They're not just theories, Sophia. They're warnings."

Sophia's stomach churned. "Warnings? Warnings about what?"

"About the entities that exist in the rift," Alex said, his voice low, a dark understanding settling in his tone. "The watchers aren't just passive observers. They're entities that manipulate the rift. They've been there since the beginning, watching those who try to cross into different realities. And they don't want anyone to alter the fabric of time."

A cold shiver ran down Sophia's spine. "So, they're not just studying the rift. They're trying to stop anyone from using it."

Alex nodded grimly. "Exactly. And if your father's research was even partially successful, it means he's meddled with something he doesn't understand. And now, we're paying the price for it."

Sophia felt the weight of the revelation sink into her chest, the reality of what they were up against becoming clearer with every passing second. She had always thought of her father as a brilliant but distant man, someone who was dedicated to his work, maybe even obsessed with it. But now she saw him differently. His obsession had put them all at risk. And as much as she hated to admit it, part of her wondered if he had known exactly what he was doing all along.

"So, what do we do now?" she asked, her voice steadier than she felt. "If these 'watchers' are real, how do we stop them?"

Alex's eyes narrowed as he leaned over the table, scanning the papers with a mix of apprehension and determination. "We don't stop them, not directly. What we need to do is understand how the rift works and how your father's research ties into it. If we can find the original data he used, the control mechanism for the rift, we might be able to close it before it destabilizes everything."

Sophia bit her lip, trying to keep her panic at bay. "But we don't even know where to look. Your research—it's all over the place."

"I know." Alex's voice was tinged with frustration, but his eyes held something deeper—an unspoken promise. "But there's one place left. One place where we can find the missing pieces. Your father's old lab."

Sophia froze. "The lab?"

Alex nodded. "It's been sealed off for years, but there's still a chance we can get inside. It's the only place where the most critical data would be kept. Your father wasn't going to leave everything to chance. He would have hidden the most important details in there."

A knot tightened in Sophia's stomach. The lab had always been a place of mystery to her. It was where her father had worked late into the night, obsessively focused on his experiments. He had always kept her away from it, telling her that it was too dangerous for her to get involved. But now, she understood why. He had known the risks—had understood them better than anyone—and yet he had pressed forward, determined to unlock the secrets of the rift.

She had to stop him. She had to stop the company. She had to stop the watchers.

"How do we get in?" she asked, her voice barely above a whisper.

"There's an entrance—hidden, deep in the company's headquarters. It's not easy to access, but it's there. And I know how to get us inside."

Sophia's heart raced at the thought. This was it—the moment they would finally take the fight to the heart of the company. The place where everything had started. The place where her father had built the machine that had opened the rift.

"And the watchers?" she asked, her voice trembling slightly. "What if they're there?"

Alex met her gaze, his eyes steady and resolute. "We'll have to deal with that once we're inside. But we can't stop now. We have to close the rift before it's too late."

Sophia felt the weight of his words settle in her chest. They

The Tipping Point

had no idea what they were up against—no idea what might be waiting for them inside her father's lab. But there was no turning back now. They couldn't afford to wait. The rift was opening, the watchers were closing in, and everything Sophia had worked to uncover was about to reach its breaking point.

She took a deep breath, steadying herself. "Then let's go," she said, her voice strong and determined.

Alex didn't hesitate. Without another word, he grabbed the map from the table, carefully folding it and slipping it into his jacket pocket. He moved toward the door, his movements swift and purposeful.

Sophia followed him, her heart racing as they stepped out into the night. The air was cool and crisp, the sky above them a blanket of stars. They had no time to waste. The rift was only growing more unstable, and with every second they spent waiting, they were putting the entire world at risk.

They walked in silence, the weight of their mission pressing down on them like a storm cloud. Sophia's thoughts flickered to the past, to the man her father had been, to the choices he had made. Had he known the consequences of his actions? Had he understood the danger of what he had unlocked?

And what about the watchers? What were they really capable of? She had a sinking feeling that the answer was something far darker than she could imagine. But they had no choice. They had to stop it.

The path ahead was uncertain, but one thing was clear: the fabric of time itself was unraveling, and they were the only ones who could put it back together.

Thirteen

Letting Go of the Past

The night air hung heavy as they moved through the quiet streets, their footsteps muffled by the weight of the darkness. Every creak of the floorboards beneath their feet, every gust of wind that rattled the windows, felt like a warning. As if the universe itself was holding its breath, waiting for the inevitable moment when the entire world would tilt on its axis, when the truth of the rift would come crashing down.

Sophia's heart pounded in her chest as she followed Alex, her breath coming in shallow bursts, her mind spinning with the knowledge of what they were about to face. Her father's lab—the heart of the company's most dangerous secret—was only a few blocks away. The thought of stepping inside that place, a place filled with memories she had spent years trying to bury, filled her with dread. But there was no turning back now. She had to face what had been hidden from her, what had been buried beneath layers of lies and secrecy.

Alex's face was set in grim determination as he led the way. His jaw was clenched, his eyes darting around as if expecting danger to leap out of the shadows. They moved quickly, purposefully, their pace quickening as they neared the entrance to the old building where her father had once worked. The building loomed ahead, its silhouette sharp against the night sky, its windows dark and empty, as if it were a hollow shell, a monument to the sins it had witnessed.

Sophia's breath caught in her throat as they approached the back entrance, the one Alex had told her about, the hidden door that no one knew about except for him. She could feel the weight of it pressing on her, the air thick with anticipation. They had no idea what lay inside, no idea what kind of dangers awaited them.

"This is it," Alex said softly, his voice barely a whisper as he stopped in front of the door. "You ready?"

Sophia nodded, but the truth was, she wasn't sure if she was ready for what was to come. She wasn't sure she was ready to face her father's legacy, or to confront the forces she had unwittingly unleashed. The rift. The watchers. The truth that had been hidden for so long.

"I'm ready," she said, forcing the words past the lump in her throat.

Alex didn't say anything more. He reached into his jacket

Letting Go of the Past

pocket and pulled out a small device—a scanner, no doubt—and pressed it against the door. There was a soft click, and the door slowly creaked open. The darkness inside was suffocating, a void that seemed to reach out and pull them in. The faint scent of dust and old machinery lingered in the air, mixing with the musty smell of forgotten secrets.

Sophia took a deep breath, steeling herself as she stepped inside, following Alex into the depths of her father's lab. The place felt cold, lifeless, as though the years of abandonment had drained it of all its energy. The walls were lined with shelves filled with old equipment, monitors, and machines that she didn't recognize. Some of them were cracked and broken, others covered in layers of dust. The flickering of a dim light in the corner was the only source of illumination, casting eerie shadows that danced across the room.

They moved silently through the space, their footsteps echoing in the silence. Sophia's eyes darted from one machine to the next, her mind racing to make sense of the technology around her. It was all so familiar, yet so foreign. The things her father had worked on, the experiments he had conducted, were beyond her understanding. But they weren't beyond Alex. He moved with purpose, his hands brushing over the equipment as though he knew exactly where to go, what to look for.

Sophia's gaze landed on one of the old monitors, a screen that flickered to life as Alex touched it. The words on the screen were a blur of symbols and equations, a language that made no sense to her. But Alex seemed to understand. He typed quickly, his fingers flying over the keys, and the screen shifted, displaying a map of some sort—a map of the rift.

"There it is," Alex murmured, his voice tight with concentration. "This is where it all started. Your father's research. He found the location of the rift."

Sophia moved closer, her breath catching as she looked at the screen. The map was marked with strange symbols, lines that seemed to connect the various points across the world, each one leading to a different dimension, a different reality. The rift was like a web, stretching out and intertwining, its threads binding the fabric of the universe together in ways that made her head spin.

"It's all connected," Sophia whispered, her voice trembling. "This isn't just about time. It's about everything."

Alex nodded, his face grim. "That's what I've been trying to tell you. Your father didn't just open a rift in time. He opened a rift in reality itself. And it's starting to collapse."

Sophia's mind raced as she processed his words. The rift wasn't just a crack in time—it was a breach in the very fabric of the universe. And her father, in his obsession with power, had torn it open, not knowing—or perhaps not caring—what the consequences would be. The watchers, the strange entities that had been mentioned in her father's notes, had to be part of this. They were there, observing, manipulating, controlling.

"The watchers," Sophia said, her voice barely a whisper. "They're not just guarding the rift. They're part of it."

Letting Go of the Past

Alex's eyes darkened as he turned to her, his jaw tight with frustration. "Exactly. They've been there from the beginning, watching those who try to manipulate time and reality. They don't want anyone messing with the rift. And if they find us, they won't hesitate to stop us."

Sophia's heart pounded in her chest, her mind reeling with the implications. The watchers weren't just observers—they were enforcers. Guardians of the rift. And if they were as powerful as Alex believed, they could easily destroy everything they had worked for, every step they had taken to expose the truth.

"We have to shut it down," she said, her voice steady now, determination rising in her chest. "We have to close the rift before it tears everything apart."

Alex nodded, his eyes locked onto hers. "That's what we came here for. But we have to find the control mechanism. It's the only way to stop it."

Sophia glanced around the room, her gaze scanning the cluttered shelves. There had to be something here, something her father had left behind, something that could help them. She stepped forward, her fingers brushing across the dusty surfaces, her mind focused on the task at hand.

Suddenly, she stopped. A small device, half-hidden behind a stack of papers, caught her eye. It was a remote, a simple black box with a red button on top. The device was connected to a series of wires that led into one of the larger machines in the corner of the room. Sophia felt her pulse quicken as she picked it up, the weight of it in her hand making her feel both hopeful and terrified.

"This is it," she said, her voice tight with excitement. "This has to be the control mechanism."

Alex moved toward her, his eyes narrowing as he examined the device. "It looks like it. But if it is, we need to activate it without alerting the watchers. If they sense what we're doing, they'll come after us."

Sophia felt a wave of cold sweat wash over her as she glanced at the machine. It was massive, its surface covered in complex symbols and gauges that seemed to pulse with an unnatural energy. The rift was connected to this machine, and whatever they did next could either save them—or destroy everything.

"We don't have much time," Alex said, his voice low and tense. "We need to act now."

Sophia took a deep breath and moved to the control panel, her hands shaking as she inserted the remote into a slot on the machine. A low hum filled the room as the machine powered up, its lights flashing, its gauges spinning wildly. Sophia's heart pounded in her chest as she looked to Alex, her mind racing.

"What happens now?" she asked, her voice tight with fear.

"We press the button," Alex said simply, his eyes locked on hers. "And we hope it works."

Letting Go of the Past

Sophia nodded, her fingers hovering over the button. The world felt like it was holding its breath, waiting for her decision. She had no idea what would happen when they pressed it, but she knew one thing for certain—they had come too far to turn back now.

With a deep breath, she pressed the button.

And in that moment, everything changed.

The ground beneath their feet trembled as the machine whirred to life. The rift—a tear in the very fabric of reality—began to close, but with it came a violent backlash, a surge of energy so powerful that it ripped through the walls of the lab. Sophia was thrown back, her body slamming into the ground as the light from the rift blazed brighter than the sun.

The watchers were here.

And they weren't going to let them escape.

Fourteen

Building a Future

The world felt like it was collapsing around her. The ground beneath her feet trembled, a deep, guttural hum vibrating through the very air, shaking her to her core. It was the rift—the reality itself was reacting to the energy she and Alex had just unleashed. Sophia's ears rang with the deafening sound, a cacophony of shifting realities, crackling energy, and the eerie, distorted hum that grew louder by the second. The walls of the lab seemed to warp and bend, the air itself warping as though the room was bending under pressure.

Her body ached from the impact as she scrambled to her feet, the force of the tremors throwing her off balance. The control panel in front of her was flickering, its lights stuttering, its mechanical hum replaced by the growing sound of distortion. She glanced frantically at Alex, who was already pushing himself off the floor, his eyes wide with realization, his face streaked with dirt

Building a Future

and sweat.

"What did we do?" Sophia shouted over the cacophony, her voice barely audible above the overwhelming noise. "What's happening?"

Alex's eyes were fixed on the machine, his jaw clenched with both fear and determination. "The rift is destabilizing," he shouted back, his voice strained. "It's too late to stop it now! We've torn the fabric too far. It's too unstable. If we don't close it now, everything will collapse into itself!"

Sophia's breath hitched as she understood the gravity of what he was saying. The rift wasn't just a breach in time—it was a fracture in the very fabric of existence. She had thought they could fix it, that pushing a button would close it forever, but now she realized that she had only opened it wider, torn the seams between worlds, allowing everything to bleed through. Time was unraveling, space was bending, and the watchers—the entities that had existed in the rift—were no longer just observers. They were moving. They were coming.

The room seemed to pulse around them as the light from the rift grew brighter, too bright to look at. Sophia shielded her eyes, but the glow seemed to burn through her eyelids, as though the very light was a living thing, searching for her, searching for them. She had no idea how long they had before the rift consumed everything, before the watchers found them, before the world itself collapsed.

"We have to fix this," she said, her voice trembling. "There has to be a way to close it. We can't let it tear everything apart."

Alex nodded grimly, his face pale with the weight of their mistake. "We don't have much time. The rift won't stay open forever. We have to get to the source, to the heart of it. The only way to stop it is to reverse the flow of energy—redirect the power and close the tear from the inside."

Sophia's heart skipped a beat. "The heart of it?" she repeated. "Where is that?"

Alex pointed toward the glowing vortex at the center of the lab, where the rift's energy seemed to be converging. The light was no longer just bright—it was blinding, its force pulling at everything around it. It was a vortex, a swirling maelstrom of energy, time, and matter, all tangled together in an impossible knot. It was growing, pulling more and more of the lab into its grip, its power expanding outward, threatening to consume the entire building.

"There," Alex said, his voice taut. "The core of the rift is where the energy is concentrated. We have to get close enough to reverse the polarity and shut it down. But it's dangerous. If we get too close, we'll be pulled into the rift ourselves."

Sophia's stomach twisted as she looked at the swirling vortex. The thought of standing in the center of that energy, where time itself seemed to bend and fracture, made her skin crawl. But there was no choice. They had to stop it. They had to shut it down before everything fell apart. The world, her world, was slipping through their fingers.

Building a Future

Taking a deep breath, Sophia moved toward the center of the room, her legs shaking with the effort to stay steady. The closer she got to the rift, the stronger the pull became. She could feel the air itself twisting, vibrating around her, like the very molecules of existence were being torn apart. The fabric of time—of reality itself—was being stretched too thin, and it could break at any moment.

Alex was beside her now, his hand gripping her arm with a sense of urgency. "We don't have much time. We need to get closer," he urged.

Sophia nodded, and they both pushed forward, step by cautious step, until they reached the heart of the rift. The light was so intense now that it felt like a force of nature, a living thing, wrapping around them, bending their senses, making the world feel unstable, fractured. Sophia felt dizzy, as if she was caught in a dream where nothing was solid, where time itself had become meaningless.

And then, it happened.

A figure appeared from the swirling vortex, stepping out of the rift like a shadow in the light. Sophia froze, her heart stopping in her chest. The figure was tall and thin, its features obscured by the blinding energy, but its presence was unmistakable. The watcher.

It was no longer just an observer. It was here, in the lab with them, its presence bending the air around it like a ripple through water. Its eyes—if they could even be called eyes—glowed with an unnatural light, and its body seemed to shimmer, as though it was made of the very fabric of the rift itself.

Alex's grip tightened on Sophia's arm. "It's here," he whispered, the fear in his voice unmistakable. "It's coming for us."

Sophia's pulse raced as the watcher stepped closer, its form flickering in and out of existence, as though it was caught between realities. It reached out, its hand—no, its arm—extending impossibly long, and the air around it crackled with power. The watcher didn't speak, but its presence was suffocating, its intent clear.

They had crossed a line, and now, they were trapped.

With every ounce of strength she had left, Sophia pushed forward, ignoring the pull of the rift, the terrifying presence of the watcher. She reached out to the heart of the rift, the machine that had opened it all. Her fingers brushed against the cold metal of the control panel, and for a moment, the world seemed to freeze.

This was it. This was the moment when everything would either be fixed or everything would be lost. The watcher was close now, its dark, glowing form hovering just inches from her. Sophia could feel its cold gaze—no, not a gaze—its presence, pressing into her very soul.

"Alex!" she shouted, her voice rising above the chaos. "Now!"

Alex didn't hesitate. With one fluid motion, he slammed his

Building a Future

hand down on the emergency switch. There was a flash of light so bright that it felt like the entire world had been consumed by it. The rift screamed, a high-pitched wail that rattled the very bones of the lab.

The light intensified, and the watcher shrieked—a sound that pierced the air, bending reality itself. Its form flickered again, and in that moment, everything seemed to snap.

The pull of the rift became unbearable, and Sophia felt herself being dragged toward it, her body weightless, her vision blurred as time and space seemed to fracture around her. She looked at Alex, her hand reaching out to him, but it was too late. The rift was taking them.

And then, just as quickly as it had all begun, the world collapsed into darkness.

For a moment, there was nothing. No sound, no light, no time.

And then, she felt it. A familiar warmth, a hand gripping hers, holding her steady. She opened her eyes.

They were no longer in the lab. They were no longer in her world.

Sophia's breath caught in her throat. She was standing in a vast, empty expanse, the world around her stretched and distorted. The sky above was a swirl of colors, the ground beneath her feet a fractured mosaic of broken realities. It was like nothing she had ever seen. She could feel the weight of time itself, collapsing and reassembling around her. And standing next to her, his hand still clutching hers, was Alex.

And then, before her, something shifted.

The watcher—its form solidified, and it loomed in front of them, its presence now even more terrifying than before. It didn't speak, but its intentions were clear. It was here to make sure that they never left. They had crossed a threshold, and there was no going back.

Sophia's heart pounded in her chest. "We have to stop it," she whispered, her voice trembling with fear and resolve. "We have to stop everything."

Alex looked at her, his eyes fierce. "We will," he said. And then, without another word, he took her hand and pulled her into the unknown, where time itself was their only enemy.

The final kiss had sealed their fate. Now, the rift between realities would either tear them apart, or it would remake them—forever changed by the world they had entered.

Fifteen

A Love That Transcends

The sky above was a violent swirl of colors—blues, reds, purples, and silvers—intertwining like threads of a vast tapestry being torn apart. Sophia felt as though she was standing in the middle of a storm, the wind howling through the air, bending space and time with every gust. Every step she took seemed to alter the very fabric of reality, and the ground beneath her feet trembled as if it were alive, shifting beneath her. The atmosphere hummed with a low frequency that resonated deep within her chest, making her feel both weightless and grounded, all at once.

Alex's hand was still firmly clasped around hers, his grip strong and steady, though she could feel the tension in his body, the weight of what they had just done. They had crossed a line that neither of them could have fully understood, not until now. Standing in the center of what seemed to be a fractured dimension, they were both acutely aware of the power they had unleashed. The rift—no, the multiple rifts—had torn through reality itself. And they were inside it now, trapped between worlds that bent and folded into one another.

"Where are we?" Sophia whispered, her voice barely audible against the swirling winds, her words getting lost in the space around them. It was as if they were in a place that defied sound itself, where nothing felt quite real, and yet everything was so vivid, so intense.

Alex didn't immediately respond, his eyes scanning their surroundings, trying to make sense of the impossible landscape. "This is… the intersection of realities," he finally said, his voice a low rasp. "We're inside the rift itself. A place where all the fractured timelines converge. We shouldn't be here."

Sophia's stomach twisted, and she pulled her hand free from his, though the moment she did, she instantly regretted it. The ground beneath her feet wavered, a brief sensation of vertigo as if the very dimension was stretching and pulling apart. She quickly steadied herself, her heart pounding in her chest.

"But we are here," she said, her voice shaking. "And it's all my fault. I—"

Alex's gaze snapped to hers, his face hard, but his eyes soft with something she couldn't quite place. "No," he interrupted firmly, "this isn't your fault. We did what we had to do. But now, we have to find a way out. This place is too unstable. It's collapsing."

Sophia could feel it. She could feel the instability in the air, the crushing sense of something about to break. The entire landscape around them seemed to pulse and throb, as though the universe itself was fighting to hold its shape, but the tension was too much. Reality was being torn, one thin thread at a time.

"Is there a way back?" she asked, her voice rising in panic. "We can't stay here. We need to fix this."

Alex's gaze grew distant, his eyes narrowing as he turned to survey the space around them. He seemed to be searching for something, his mind working furiously. The air was thick with the crackle of energy, the sound of reality itself fraying at the edges. It felt like the rift wasn't just a tear—it was a wound, and they were the ones who had inflicted it.

"There's a way," Alex said quietly, after a long pause. "But we'll need to reach the core. The center of the rift. That's where it all started. Where it all connects. If we can get there and reverse the energy flow, we might be able to stabilize it."

Sophia's breath hitched at the thought. The core. She could feel it, pulling at her, an invisible force that seemed to emanate from deep within the swirling chaos around them. It was like a heartbeat, constant and insistent, a pulse that she couldn't ignore. But getting there wouldn't be easy. The very ground they stood on seemed to shift beneath them, like an ocean of jagged, unstable fragments. There were no paths, no clear way forward—just endless distortion, where nothing felt solid.

"I'm with you," she said, her voice steady despite the chaos raging inside her. "We'll do this. Together."

Alex nodded, his eyes fixed on the horizon—or whatever semblance of it there was. "We don't have much time. The longer we're here, the more unstable it becomes. The rift is collapsing, Sophia. And if we don't get to the core soon, everything will implode. It will tear through every reality, through every timeline… and it will destroy everything."

Sophia swallowed hard. The gravity of his words sank in. She hadn't just opened a rift in time. She had opened a doorway to multiple dimensions, multiple versions of the world, each one fragile and teetering on the brink of destruction. She had never imagined the power she had unleashed. Never realized how far-reaching the consequences would be.

Taking a deep breath, she squared her shoulders. "Then we need to move, now."

Together, they began walking through the fractured landscape, navigating the unstable ground as best they could. The world around them twisted and warped with each step, the ground shifting underfoot like a living thing. At times, the very air felt thick, as though it were made of liquid, and every movement felt like it took more effort than it should have. Reality was breaking apart, and it was dragging them along with it.

Sophia couldn't shake the sensation of being watched. There were no clear signs—no eyes, no shapes, but the feeling lingered. It was as if something was moving just beyond the edges of perception, something that was aware of their every move, something waiting for them to make a mistake.

"They're here," Alex muttered, his voice laced with urgency.

Sophia's heart skipped a beat. "The watchers?"

Alex didn't answer, but his pace quickened, his steps more urgent now. Sophia tried to keep up, but the ground beneath her feet seemed to move faster, the cracks widening, the air growing heavier with each passing moment. And then she saw them.

The watchers.

They weren't human. They weren't anything she could recognize. Their forms seemed to flicker between dimensions, like shadows cast from another reality. They were tall and formless, their bodies shifting in and out of focus, their eyes glowing with an unnatural light that pierced through the distorted space around them.

Sophia froze, a cold chill creeping down her spine. She could feel their gaze on her, though they didn't have eyes—just the endless, all-consuming light that seemed to see straight through her. There were no words, no sound, but the pressure was suffocating. It was as if the very fabric of the rift was alive with their presence, and it was this presence that was causing everything to tear.

Alex was already moving again, pulling her forward, but the watchers weren't giving up that easily. They were closing in, their forms flickering with increasing speed, moving like shadows in a broken mirror.

"They won't stop," Alex said, his voice tight. "We have to keep moving, no matter what."

Sophia's breath quickened as they ran, the watchers following them, always a few steps behind, but their presence growing stronger with each passing second. She could feel their energy, their power, pressing in on her from all sides. They weren't just following—they were guiding them, pushing them toward something.

Toward the center.

Sophia's heart pounded, but she didn't dare stop. Not now. Not when they were so close. The ground beneath her feet shifted again, and she almost stumbled, but Alex caught her arm, steadying her.

"Hold on," he said, his voice low but intense. "We're almost there."

And then, they reached it. The center of the rift. The heart of the chaos.

Before them stood a structure—ancient, impossibly vast, and built from the same unstable energy that surrounded them. It looked like a tower, but it was made of shifting light and solid darkness, its form constantly shifting, as though it existed in a place between places. It was the core, the nexus point of everything, and it was this structure that held the power to either fix the rift—or tear it apart forever.

Alex pulled a small device from his pocket, something that looked almost like a key, but as he approached the structure, he froze. His face went pale, his hand trembling slightly as he raised the key toward the tower.

"They know," he whispered.

Sophia looked around, panic rising in her chest. The watchers were here, all around them, their forms flickering faster now, their presence suffocating, their intentions clear. They weren't here to stop the rift from collapsing—they were here to stop them from closing it.

"We don't have a choice," Sophia said, her voice breaking through the tension. "We have to close it. Now."

Alex looked at her, his eyes filled with fear and resolve. "Are you ready for this?"

Sophia nodded. "We don't have another option."

With one last glance at the watchers closing in on them, Alex inserted the key into the structure. The world around them seemed to hold its breath, the very fabric of the rift crackling with tension as the energy began to shift. The watchers screamed—a sound that pierced the air, a sound that rattled her very bones.

Then, everything went black.

Time shattered.

www.ingramcontent.com/pod-product-compliance
Lightning Source LLC
LaVergne TN
LVHW020423080526
838202LV00055B/5018